HAL•LEONARD

pro vocal®
BETTER THAN KARAOKE!

SONGBOOK & SOUND-ALIKE CD
WITH UNIQUE *PITCH-CHANGER*™

MEN'S EDITION
VOLUME 22

Great Standards

T0081515

ISBN 978-1-4234-2189-4

HAL•LEONARD®
CORPORATION
7777 W. BLUEMOUND RD. P.O. BOX 13819 MILWAUKEE, WI 53213

Visit Hal Leonard Online at
www.halleonard.com

CONTENTS

Beyond the Sea

Music by Charles Louis Trenet and Albert Abraham Lasry
French Lyrics by Charles Louis Trenet
English Lyrics by Jack Lawrence

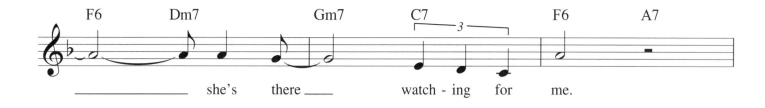

she's there _____ watch - ing for me.

If I _____ could fly _____ like bird on high, _____

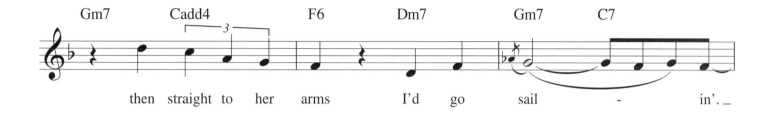

then straight to her arms I'd go sail - in'. _____

Bridge

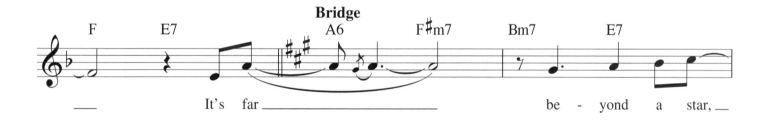

_____ It's far _____ be - yond a star, _____

_____ it's near _____ be - yond a moon. _____

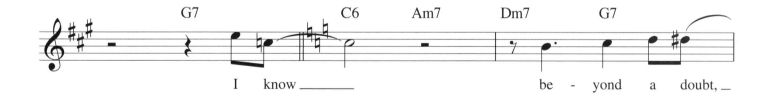

I know _____ be - yond a doubt, _____

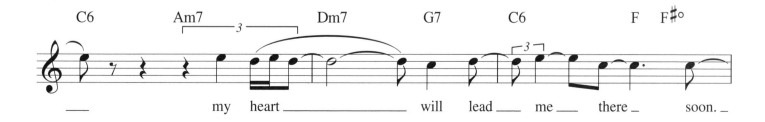

_____ my heart _____ will lead _____ me _____ there _____ soon. _____

Blame It on My Youth

Words by Edward Heyman
Music by Oscar Levant

For All We Know

Words by Sam M. Lewis
Music by J. Fred Coots

Verse

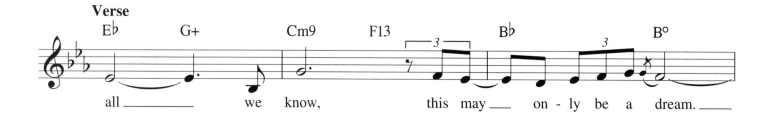

all _____ we know, this may ___ on - ly be a dream. ___

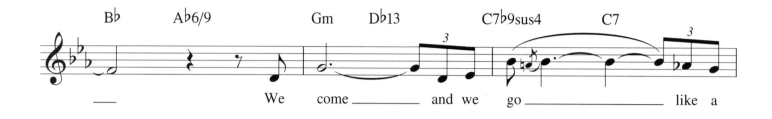

___ We come _____ and we go _____ like a

rip - ple on a stream. _____ So love me _____ to -

night, to - mor - row was made for ___ some. ___ To -

mor - row may ___ nev - er come, ___ for all we know. _____

Outro
Slower, rubato

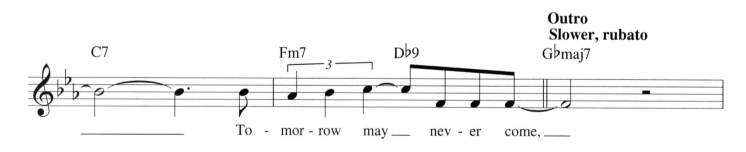

_____ To - mor - row may ___ nev - er come, ___

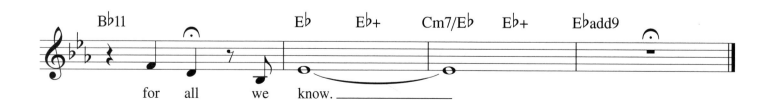

for all we know. _____

12

I Don't Know Why
(I Just Do)

Lyric by Roy Turk
Music by Fred E. Ahlert

13

I Left My Heart in San Francisco

Words by Douglass Cross
Music by George Cory

- cis - co. ___ High ___ on a hill,

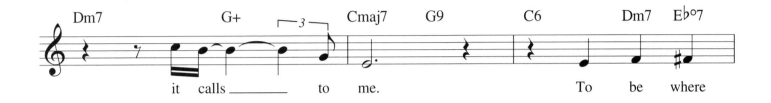

it calls _____ to me. To be where

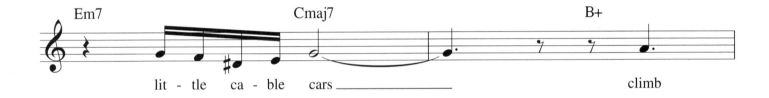

lit - tle ca - ble cars _____ climb

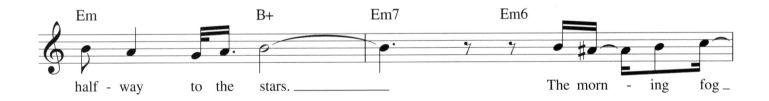

half - way to the stars. _____ The morn - ing fog ___

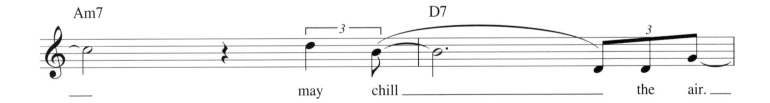

___ may chill _____ the air. ___

___ I ___ don't ___ care, ___ My love waits there ___

The Way You Look Tonight

Words by Dorothy Fields
Music by Jerome Kern

What a Wonderful World

Words and Music by George David Weiss and Bob Thiele

They're real - ly say - in', "I love you." I hear ba - bies cry, _____ I watch them grow. _____ They'll learn much _____ more than I'll _____ ev - er know, _____ and I think to my - self, _____ "What a won - der - ful world." _____

Yes, _____ I think to my - self, _____ "What a won - der - ful world." _____ Oh, _____ yeah.

Where or When

from BABES IN ARMS
Words by Lorenz Hart
Music by Richard Rodgers

Pro Vocal® Series
SONGBOOK & SOUND-ALIKE CD
SING 8 GREAT SONGS
WITH A PROFESSIONAL BAND

Whether you're a karaoke singer or an auditioning professional, the Pro Vocal® series is for you! Unlike most karaoke packs, each book in the Pro Vocal Series contains the lyrics, melody, and chord symbols for eight hit songs. The CD contains demos for listening, and separate backing tracks so you can sing along. The CD is playable on any CD player, but it is also enhanced so PC and Mac computer users can adjust the recording to any pitch without changing the tempo! Perfect for home rehearsal, parties, auditions, corporate events, and gigs without a backup band.

WOMEN'S EDITIONS

MEN'S EDITIONS

MIXED EDITIONS

These editions feature songs for both male and female voices.

FOR MORE INFORMATION, SEE YOUR LOCAL MUSIC DEALER, OR WRITE TO:

HAL•LEONARD®
CORPORATION
7777 W. BLUEMOUND RD. P.O. BOX 13819 MILWAUKEE, WI 53213

Visit Hal Leonard online at www.halleonard.com

Prices, contents, & availability subject to change without notice.
Disney charaters and artwork © Disney Enterprises, Inc.

0310

SING WITH THE CHOIR

CD INCLUDED

These GREAT COLLECTIONS let singers
BECOME PART OF A FULL CHOIR and sing along
with some of the most-loved songs of all time.

Each book includes SATB parts (arrangements are enlarged from octavo-size to 9" x 12")
and the accompanying CD features full, professionally recorded performances.

Now you just need to turn on the CD, open the book, pick your part, and
SING ALONG WITH THE CHOIR!

1. ANDREW LLOYD WEBBER

Any Dream Will Do • As If We Never Said Good-bye • Don't Cry for Me Argentina • Love Changes Everything • Memory • The Music of the Night • Pie Jesu • Whistle down the Wind.
00333001 Book/CD Pack................................. $14.95

2. BROADWAY

Bring Him Home • Cabaret • For Good • Luck Be a Lady • Seasons of Love • There's No Business like Show Business • Where Is Love? • You'll Never Walk Alone.
00333002 Book/CD Pack................................. $14.95

3. STANDARDS

Cheek to Cheek • Georgia on My Mind • I Left My Heart in San Francisco • I'm Beginning to See the Light • Moon River • On the Sunny Side of the Street • Skylark • When I Fall in Love.
00333003 Book/CD Pack................................. $14.95

4. THE 1950s

At the Hop • The Great Pretender • Kansas City • La Bamba • Love Me Tender • My Prayer • Rock Around the Clock • Unchained Melody.
00333004 Book/CD Pack................................. $14.95

5. THE 1960s

All You Need is Love • Can't Help Falling in Love • Dancing in the Street • Good Vibrations • I Heard It Through the Grapevine • I'm a Believer • Under the Boardwalk • What a Wonderful World.
00333005 Book/CD Pack................................. $14.95

6. THE 1970s

Ain't No Mountain High Enough • Bohemian Rhapsody • I'll Be There • Imagine • Let It Be • Night Fever • Yesterday Once More • You Are the Sunshine of My Life.
00333006 Book/CD Pack................................. $14.95

7. DISNEY FAVORITES

The Bare Necessities • Be Our Guest • Circle of Life • Cruella De Vil • Friend like Me • Hakuna Matata • Joyful, Joyful • Under the Sea.
00333007 Book/CD Pack................................. $14.95

8. DISNEY HITS

Beauty and the Beast • Breaking Free • Can You Feel the Love Tonight • Candle on the Water • Colors of the Wind • A Whole New World (Aladdin's Theme) • You'll Be in My Heart • You've Got a Friend in Me.
00333008 Book/CD Pack................................. $14.95

9. LES MISÉRABLES

At the End of the Day • Bring Him Home • Castle on a Cloud • Do You Hear the People Sing? • Finale • I Dreamed a Dream • On My Own • One Day More.
00333009 Book/CD Pack................................. $14.99

10. CHRISTMAS FAVORITES

Frosty the Snow Man • The Holiday Season • (There's No Place Like) Home for the Holidays • Little Saint Nick • Merry Christmas, Darling • Santa Claus Is Comin' to Town • Silver Bells • White Christmas.
00333011 Book/CD Pack................................. $14.95

11. CHRISTMAS TIME IS HERE

Blue Christmas • Christmas Time is Here • Feliz Navidad • Happy Xmas (War Is Over) • I'll Be Home for Christmas • Let It Snow! Let It Snow! Let It Snow! • We Need a Little Christmas • Wonderful Christmastime.
00333012 Book/CD Pack................................. $14.95

12. THE SOUND OF MUSIC

Climb Ev'ry Mountain • Do-Re-Mi • Edelweiss • The Lonely Goatherd • My Favorite Things • So Long, Farewell • The Sound of Music.
00333019 Book/CD Pack................................. $14.99

13. CHRISTMAS CAROLS

Angels We Have Heard on High • Deck the Hall • Go, Tell It on the Mountain • Joy to the World • O Come, All Ye Faithful (Adeste Fideles) • O Holy Night • Silent Night • We Wish You a Merry Christmas.
00333020 Book/CD Pack................................. $14.99

14. GLEE

Can't Fight This Feeling • Don't Stop Believin' • Jump • Keep Holding On • Lean on Me • No Air • Rehab • Somebody to Love.
00333059 Book/CD Pack................................. $16.99

FOR MORE INFORMATION, SEE YOUR LOCAL MUSIC DEALER, OR WRITE TO:

HAL•LEONARD® CORPORATION
7777 W. BLUEMOUND RD. P.O. BOX 13819 MILWAUKEE, WI 53213

Prices, contents, and availability
subject to change without notice.